WHAT DOES A
RECEIVER
DO?

Paul Challen

PowerKiDS press
New York

Published in 2015 by The Rosen Publishing Group, Inc.
29 East 21st Street, New York, NY 10010

Produced for Rosen by BlueApple*Works* Inc.
Art Director: Tibor Choleva
Designer: Joshua Avramson
Photo Research: Jane Reid
Editor for BlueApple*Works*: Melissa McClellan
US Editor: Joshua Shadowens

Photo Credits: Cover, p. 14 Susan Leggett/Shutterstock; p. 1, 8 James Boardman/Dreamstime;
p. 3 Alhovik/Shutterstock, background Bruno Ferrari/Shutterstock; p. 4, 17 Aspen Photo/
Shutterstock; p. 5, 9, 10, 11, 15, 16, 18, 20, 29 Andy Cruz; p. 6 Lawrence Weslowski Jr/
Dreamstime; p. 7 Ruth Peterkin/Dreamstime; p. 12 Michael A. Lantron, USN/public domain;
p. 13 Mike Liu/Shutterstock; p. 19 Peter Weber/Shutterstock; p. 21, 27 bottom Mark Herreid/
Dreamstime; p. 22 Jason Tench/Shutterstock; p. 23 Eric Broder Van Dyke/Shutterstock; p. 24
Jcpjr/Dreamstime; p. 25 Ken Cole/Dreamstime; p. 26 left Sharp2905/Bigstock; p. 26 right Scott
Anderson/Dreamstime; p. 27 top Jerry Coli/Dreamstime; p. 28 Richard Thornton/Shutterstock

Library of Congress Cataloging-in-Publication Data

Challen, Paul C. (Paul Clarence), 1967–
 What does a receiver do? / by Paul Challen.
    pages cm. — (Football smarts)
 Includes index.
 ISBN 978-1-4777-7002-3 (library binding) — ISBN 978-1-4777-7003-0 (pbk.) —
 ISBN 978-1-4777-7004-7 (6-pack)
 1. End play (Football)—Juvenile literature. 2. Wide receivers (Football)—Juvenile literature. 3.
Tight ends (Football)—Juvenile literature. I. Title.
 GV951.25.C47 2015
 796.332'2—dc23
                                      2014001253

Manufactured in the United States of America

CPSIA Compliance Information: Batch #WS14PK8 For Further Information contact: Rosen Publishing, New York, New York at 1-800-237-9932

TABLE OF CONTENTS

THE FOOTBALL TEAM

A football team is really two separate teams, an **offense** and a **defense**. No team can be successful without both sides being at the top of their game. A football team's offense and defense are made up of several positions. All of these positions come together to make a strong defensive and offensive unit. Balancing offensive and defensive strength is key to having a good team.

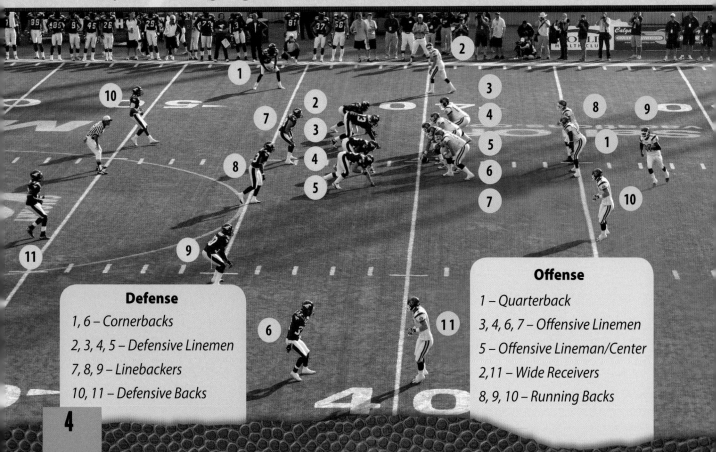

Defense

1, 6 – Cornerbacks

2, 3, 4, 5 – Defensive Linemen

7, 8, 9 – Linebackers

10, 11 – Defensive Backs

Offense

1 – Quarterback

3, 4, 6, 7 – Offensive Linemen

5 – Offensive Lineman/Center

2, 11 – Wide Receivers

8, 9, 10 – Running Backs

The receiver is an offensive player. The receiver on a football team is the player responsible for catching passes, and trying to run with the ball when it is passed. He also blocks for his teammates. To play this position, you have to be a great athlete, and you must understand the game very well. Receivers must be strong and agile, and able to catch passes with confidence.

When a team looks to move the ball with passing plays, it is the receiver (marked with arrows throughout this book) who often makes the catch from a ball thrown by the quarterback.

STRATEGY

When a football team has the ball, the offense must move it down the field using running or passing plays, and attempt to score a **touchdown** or kick a **field goal**. The defense tries to stop them. Both sides face off at the **line of scrimmage** on each play in a game.

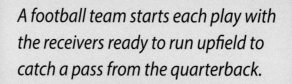

A football team starts each play with the receivers ready to run upfield to catch a pass from the quarterback.

Receivers have to communicate well with their quarterbacks. The coach or offensive **coordinator** usually calls the plays a team will run on offense, and the receiver has to know his role in every play. Also, the receiver must be able to "read" a defense, before a play begins. If he sees defensive players lined up in unexpected ways, he has to change his run off the line of scrimmage.

Understanding how to get past defensive players is a key part of being a good receiver.

THE RIGHT STANCE

To be able to explode off the line of scrimmage, receivers need to get set in the right **stance** before the ball is snapped. The two-point stance is the most common, as receivers place one foot in front and one in back, with the knees bent and a slight forward lean.

A player gets into a two-point stance. The only requirement for a two-point stance is that both feet touch the ground at the same time. Though the actual stance will vary depending on the player and the position, getting into a two-point stance is relatively easy.

The names of the stances tell how many times a player's body touches the ground in each stance. In a two-point stance, both feet touch the ground. In a three-point stance, both feet and one hand touch the ground, and a four-point stance uses both feet and both hands. A player's stance can give him an edge over an **opponent** that stands in the way.

Many offensive plays are also designed for receivers to start "in motion"—that is, running parallel to the line of scrimmage. When the ball is snapped, they change direction and head upfield. It's important not to cross the line of scrimmage before the **snap**, though, or the receiver will be called **offside**.

Receivers need to be ready to sprint off the line of scrimmage when the ball is snapped.

PERFECT RELEASE

The rules of the game allow the defensive player to make contact with the receiver as he leaves the line of scrimmage. This "bump" makes it hard for a receiver to build up speed and get open for a catch. That's why it's important for receivers to perfect their release from a defensive player.

In good bump and run coverage, the defensive player will make a good bump on the offensive player in the first five yards. Teammates often come to help their receiver when they see him getting bumped .

When he leaves the line of scrimmage, an experienced receiver will continue to move his feet on contact with the defender. He will push off his opponent with his hands, moving to one side to get past the defender. Having an effective release is a big part of being a receiver because without it, you'll be stopped at the line every time!

Being bumped by the defense can prevent the receivers from running downfield quickly. A receiver needs to be able to get past the defensive player's first bump and head upfield to catch a pass. It takes strength and speed to do this well.

FIELD ZONES

As a team's receivers line up and get ready for the snap, they look at the field in front of them in three basic zones— short, medium, and deep.

During passing plays the receivers will run downfield to the zone that the play has called for. This can cause one or more receivers to become open, and give the quarterback a good target for a successful pass. The ultimate goal of a receiver after he catches the ball is to enter the end zone and score a touchdown.

As part of a team's offensive **strategy**, they will run routes into any or all of these zone to make a catch. Generally speaking, the short zone is the section of the field that's up to 5 yards in front of scrimmage. The medium zone is from 5 to about 12 yards—and the deep zone is anything farther than that. Teams pass into the three kinds of zones depending on how many yards they need to gain and how the opposing defense sets up.

Short Zone – Purple Area
Medium Zone – Yellow Area
Deep Zone – Blue Area
End Zone – Orange Area

A team scores a touchdown by entering its opponent's end zone while carrying the ball or catching the ball while being within the end zone.

THREE TYPES OF PASSES

There are basically three types of passes a receiver can catch —short, medium, and long. Sometimes, a team will need short yardage, so a receiver will be assigned to run into the short zone and look for a quick pass from the quarterback.

The receiver must be able to catch the ball in crowded situations with many defensive players trying to stop him.

Other times, a team will need more yards, so the play will call for receivers to run into the medium or deep zones to make the catch. With all of these passes it is important to remember that good receivers can keep going after the ball is caught—avoiding **tackles** and gaining more yards!

Once they are past defensive players, the receivers must run fast to gain yards for their team. A team that is unable to move the ball consistently will have difficulty winning games. A play where the ball is moved upfield by 15 yards or more is called a "big play."

GETTING OPEN

The pass route is the path a receiver will take once the ball is snapped, as he tries to get open for a catch. These routes are almost always pre-planned, and offensive passing plays have several different receivers all running different routes.

An offensive team will have receivers running many different pass routes. It's very important that all these players know what routes to run—and what their teammates will be doing as well!

Running an effective route is not all about the receiver, though. He has to cooperate closely with the quarterback so that both players know in advance which routes are going to be executed. With several receivers running routes on any given play, it's important to avoid a collision.

Running a successful pass route can lead to touchdowns!

SHORT ROUTES

Receivers need to be fast and agile to be successful in executing short routes. Often, they require only a few quick strides before the quarterback throws them the ball, so being sure-handed is also crucial!

The short passing game is a great way for a team to move the ball and gain yardage.

One common short route is the quick out. On this play the receiver runs a few yards, then cuts quickly to the left or right, "out" to the sideline. Another short route is the hitch. On this play the receiver runs out a few yards, and stops and turns quickly to catch a short pass. On the slant, a third type of short route, the receiver runs diagonal to the line of scrimmage and looks for a carefully thrown ball by the quarterback after just a few strides.

A receiver doesn't just make up what he does with the football. All of a team's plays are written down in a playbook that tells the offense, defense, and special teams what plays can be called in any situation. The playbook is so important that a player must give his back if he leaves the team! The team does not want any opponents to learn about the plays.

MEDIUM ROUTES

As the name suggests, receivers run medium routes to help their team gain anywhere from about 5 to 12 yards from the line of scrimmage. Because the medium zone is often flooded with defensive players like linebackers and defensive backs, receivers have to be very careful in this area— it's easy to get hit!

A receiver has to watch for the pass defenders. Pass defenders play the important role of keeping passes from being completed downfield. They try to keep the ball away from the receiver. A pass defender may even catch the ball himself. This is called an interception.

"Busted play" describes a play that fails right after the snap. Usually this is caused by a misunderstanding about the play call. A busted play often happens when a quarterback tries to hand the ball to a running back who is running a different play. A fumble or loss of yards may result.

One example of a common medium route is the hook. On this play, the receiver runs straight off the line of scrimmage and then, similar to the hitch pattern, makes a quick turn to catch the pass. The hook is really just another name for a medium-length hitch. Another common medium route is the out. Again, this is like the quick out play, but this time the receiver runs farther off the line of scrimmage, and then out to the sideline.

The sidelines are the thick white lines which mark the boundaries of a sports field.

DEEP ROUTES

When a team needs big yardage, deep routes can produce some of the most exciting plays in football. When a receiver sprints past the man covering him and the quarterback tosses the "long bomb," fans get up and cheer!

On a passing play, the quarterback has to drop back, decide which receiver has the best chance of catching the ball, then throw the ball before the defense can sack him.

On one deep zone route, the receiver sprints off the line and heads deep into opposing territory. He tries to outrun the defensive player covering him, and as he gets past him, the quarterback aims the ball into the space where the receiver will be. A comeback route begins just like an up pattern, but instead of trying to sprint past the defensive player, the receiver angles back, or makes a "comeback" towards the quarterback, who throws the ball to him.

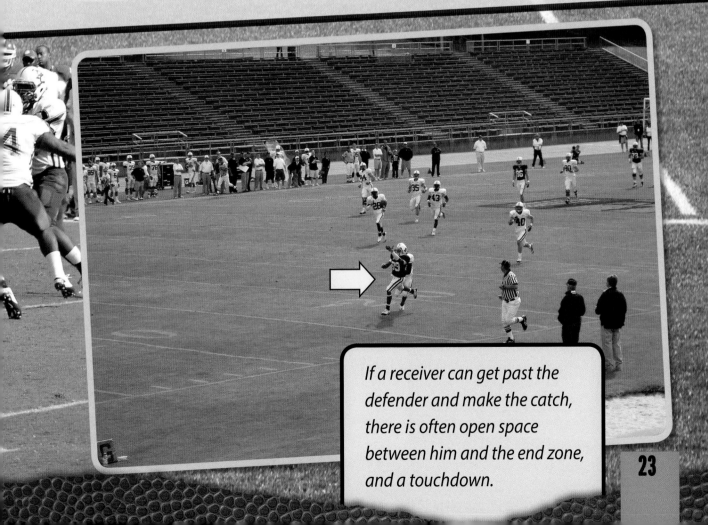

If a receiver can get past the defender and make the catch, there is often open space between him and the end zone, and a touchdown.

THE ROLE OF A COACH

A football coach is the person in charge of the entire team, from the offense to the defense and the entire coaching staff. He calls the plays from the sidelines, and determines before the game how his team will approach a given rival.

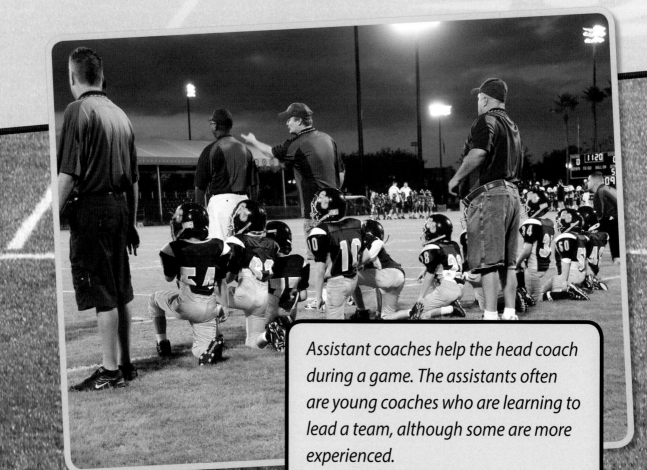

Assistant coaches help the head coach during a game. The assistants often are young coaches who are learning to lead a team, although some are more experienced.

Most coaches don't work alone, though. They are assisted by other coaches who specialize in certain aspects of the game, like working with quarterbacks, defensive backs, or scouting opponents. The two main assistants are the offensive and defensive play coordinators.

Play coordinators go over strategy with players. There is one play coordinator for offense and another for defense. They often are responsible for making the team's game plan and explaining it to the players.

THE BEST RECEIVERS

Some of the fastest, most exciting players in the history of the game have been receivers. Steve Largent of the Seattle Seahawks, Terrell Owens who played for six NFL teams during his career, Cris Carter and Randy Moss, both of the Minnesota Vikings, and Andre Reed of the Buffalo Bills were all skilled, fearless receivers who helped their teams pack a powerful offensive punch.

Calvin Johnson (left), wide receiver for the Detroit Lions, is big, fast, and agile. His nickname is Megatron.

Larry Fitzgerald (right), wide receiver for the Arizona Cardinals, is one of the best receivers playing today.

In recent years, A.J. Green, Brandon Marshall, Andre Johnson, and Dez Bryant have all been outstanding receivers and big-time fan favorites.

Jordy Nelson, the standout receiver of the Green Bay Packers, was also an excellent track and field athlete when he was in high school.

BE A GOOD SPORT

Any pro coach or player will tell you that sportsmanship is a vital part of football. Of course, the pros play as hard as they can to win, but they remember that respect for teammates, opponents, coaches, **referees**, and fans is also very important—just like playing fair.

Learning about good sportsmanship starts at practice sessions.

Football has a set of rules that clearly draws a line between fair and unfair play. These rules are set to keep players safe and to provide structure to the game itself. Hitting and blocking cleanly, following the rules, and shaking hands after a game are all a big part of being a good sport. If everyone remembers to treat one another with respect, the game of football can only come out a winner!

Throughout October many football players, including NFL players, wear pink socks or other accessories for Breast Cancer Awareness month.

GLOSSARY

coordinator
(koh-WOR-duh-nay-tur)
A person who organizes the
activities of others.

defense (DEE-fents) A group of
players trying to stop points from
being scored by the other team.

field goal (FEELD GOHL) A play
worth 3 points in which the ball
is kicked through the uprights
of the goalpost.

line of scrimmage
(LYN UV SKRIH-mij) The invisible
line where the ball was last down
and where the next play starts.

offense (O-fents) A group of
players trying to score points for
their team.

offside (AHF-syd) The rules call
for both teams to stay on their side
of the line of scrimmage before the
ball is snapped. An offside penalty
is called when a player moves
before the ball is snapped.

opponent (uh-POH-nunt) A
person you are competing against
in a game.

referees (reh-fuh-REEZ) Officials
in charge of the game.

snap (SNAP) The action of the
center tossing the ball between his
legs to the quarterback.

stance (STANS) A way
of standing.

strategy (STRA-tuh-jee) A type
of clever plan.

tackles (TA-kuls) Knocks down
or throws another player to
the ground.

touchdown (TUTCH-down)
A play worth six points when a
player carries or catches the ball
in their opponents' end zone.

FOR MORE INFORMATION

FURTHER READING

Edwards, Ethan. *Meet Calvin Johnson: Football's Megatron*. All-Star Players. New York: PowerKids Press, 2014.

Gigliotti, Jim. *Receivers*. Game Day: Football. New York: Gareth Stevens, 2010.

Hurley, Michael. *Football*. Fantastic Sports Facts. Mankato, MN: Capstone Press, 2013.

WEBSITES

Due to the changing nature of Internet links, PowerKids Press has developed an online list of websites related to the subject of this book. This site is updated regularly. Please use this link to access the list:

www.powerkidslinks.com/fbs/rece/

INDEX